Poseidon

BY VIRGINIA LOH-HAGAN

Gods and goddesses were the main characters of myths. Myths are traditional stories from ancient cultures. Storytellers answered questions about the world by creating exciting explanations. People thought myths were true. Myths explained the unexplainable. They helped people make sense of human behavior and nature. Today, we use science to explain the world. But people still love myths. Myths may not be literally true. But they have meaning. They tell us something about our history and culture.

45th Parallel Press

Published in the United States of America by Cherry Lake Publishing
Ann Arbor, Michigan
www.cherrylakepublishing.com

Content Adviser: Matthew Wellenbach, Catholic Memorial School, West Roxbury, MA
Reading Adviser: Marla Conn MS, Ed., Literacy specialist, Read-Ability, Inc.
Book Designer: Jen Wahi

Photo Credits: © Miroslav Trifonov/Shutterstock.com, 5; © Samot/Shutterstock.com, 6; © Howard David Johnson, 2016, 8; © graf/istockphoto.com, 11; © Galushko Sergey/Shutterstock.com, 13; © Aelice/Shutterstock.com, 15; © Kira Makohon/Shutterstock.com, 17; © tsuneomp/Shutterstock.com, 19; © Fer Gregory/Shutterstock.com, 21; © Katja Gerasimova/Shutterstock.com, 22; © Algol/Shutterstock.com, 25; © Zwiebackesser/Shutterstock.com, 27; © Sergei Afanasev/Shutterstock.com, 29; © Howard David Johnson, 2016, Cover; various art elements throughout, shutterstock.com

45th Parallel Press is an imprint of Cherry Lake Publishing.

Library of Congress Cataloging-in-Publication Data

Names: Loh-Hagan, Virginia, author.
Title: Poseidon / by Virginia Loh-Hagan.
Description: Ann Arbor : Cherry Lake Publishing, [2017] | Series: Gods and
  goddesses of the ancient world | Includes bibliographical references and
  index.
Identifiers: LCCN 2016031221| ISBN 9781634721332 (hardcover) | ISBN
  9781634722650 (pbk.) | ISBN 9781634721998 (pdf) | ISBN 9781634723312
  (ebook)
Subjects: LCSH: Poseidon (Greek deity)--Juvenile literature. | Gods,
  Greek--Juvenile literature. | Mythology, Greek--Juvenile literature.
Classification: LCC BL820.N5 L64 2017 | DDC 292.2/113--dc23
LC record available at https://lccn.loc.gov/2016031221

Printed in the United States of America
Corporate Graphics

ABOUT THE AUTHOR:

Dr. Virginia Loh-Hagan is an author, university professor, former classroom teacher, and curriculum designer. She loves mermaids and sea animals. She lives in San Diego with her very tall husband and very naughty dogs. To learn more about her, visit www.virginialoh.com.

TABLE OF CONTENTS

CHAPTER 1

UNDER THE SEA

Who is Poseidon? How was he born? How did he get his wife?

Poseidon was a Greek god. He was one of the 12 **Olympians**. These gods were the rulers of the gods. They lived on Mount Olympus. Mount Olympus is in Greece. It's the highest mountain in Greece.

Poseidon's parents were Cronus and Rhea. They were **Titans**. Titans were giant gods. They had great strength. They ruled until the Olympians took over.

Cronus was told that a son would take away his power. So, Cronus ate his children. Poseidon was one of them.

Rhea hid one child, Zeus. Later, Zeus came back. He tricked Cronus. He poisoned him. Cronus threw up Poseidon and his other children.

Zeus led a war against the Titans. Poseidon and his **siblings** won. Siblings are brothers and sisters.

Mount Olympus was the meeting place of the gods.

Poseidon, Zeus, and Hades shared power over the land and Mount Olympus.

They divided the world into three main parts. The three most powerful Olympians ruled them. Zeus was the god of the sky. Hades was the god of the underworld. Poseidon was the god of the seas. They were brothers. So, they would fight. They fought for power.

Poseidon mainly lived underwater. He lived in a big castle. His castle was made of gold. He wanted a wife to live with him.

He saw Amphitrite dancing. He fell in love with her. Amphitrite was a sea **nymph**. Nymphs are beautiful spirits.

Family Tree

Grandparents: Uranus (Father Sky) and Gaia (Mother Earth)

Parents: Cronus (god of time) and Rhea (goddess of fertility)

Brothers: Zeus (god of the sky), Hades (god of the underworld)

Sisters: Hera (goddess of women and marriage), Demeter (goddess of the harvest), Hestia (goddess of the hearth and family)

Spouse: Amphitrite (sea goddess)

Children: Benthesikyme (goddess of the waves), Rhodos (goddess of the island of Rhodes), Triton (merman, messenger of the sea), also had at least 12 other children

Her father was Nereus, the Old Man of the Sea. Her mother was the daughter of Oceanus. Oceanus was a Titan. He was the "Father of the Waters."

Amphitrite didn't like Poseidon at first. She ran away from him. Poseidon searched everywhere. He was sad. He sent messengers to get her. A dolphin convinced her to marry him.

Poseidon had many lovers. He loved other goddesses, nymphs, and **mortals**. Mortals are humans. He had many children with different women. He protected his children.

 Poseidon had long, curly dark hair and a beard.

CHAPTER 2

BEYOND WATER

What are some of Poseidon's powers? How does he use his powers for good?

Poseidon had total control of the oceans. He created storms. He sank ships. He drowned lands. He drowned people. He created floods. Then, he'd create nice weather. He calmed the seas. He saved ships. He saved people. He liked causing trouble. But he liked bringing peace, too.

He created all the sea animals. He gave people seafood. He created new islands. He protected all the waters. Sailors worshipped Poseidon. They prayed to him. Poseidon gave them safe travels. He kept them alive.

He helped the land produce crops. He watered the earth. Sometimes he's called "Holder of the Earth."

Poseidon did more than control water. He was also the "Tamer of Horses." He often gave his horses as gifts. It was a great honor.

Poseidon gave life to the oceans.

All in the Family

Poseidon had a child with his sister, Demeter. Poseidon and Demeter's son was named Arion. Arion was immortal. Arion looked like a horse. But he had wings. He also had human feet. He was fast. No one in a chariot race could pass him. He used his wings to speed up. Sometimes he pulled Poseidon's chariot. Arion could speak and was very smart. He's often confused with Pegasus. Pegasus was another one of Poseidon's sons. His mother was Medusa. He was a winged horse. He was pure white. When his hoof hit the ground, a spring of water came out.

Poseidon was honorable. He kept his promises. He was honest about his feelings.

He wanted more than just the sea. He fought with Athena over a city. Athena was the goddess of wisdom. The two gods had a contest. They gave the city a gift. The city picked the best gift. That god would be the ruler.

Poseidon created a horse from sea foam. He gave it to the city. Athena gave an olive tree. Athena won. So, the city was named Athens. Poseidon got mad. He flooded the land around Athens.

CHAPTER 3

EARTH-SHAKER

Why is Poseidon feared? How does he use his powers for evil?

Poseidon could be an angry god. Ancient Greeks wanted to keep him happy. But he wasn't always happy. He was very **moody**. He changed his feelings. He was either calm or stormy. The seas reflected Poseidon's moods.

Poseidon was also known as "Earth-Shaker." Ancient Greeks believed earthquakes were caused when waters **eroded** the rocks. Erode means to wear away. Poseidon caused earthquakes. He did this when he was mad. Some people believed he turned into a bull while shaking the earth.

He had a bad **temper**. He got angry easily. He didn't like to be insulted. He took **revenge**. He got even.

Polyphemus was Poseidon's son. He was a giant. He had one eye. Odysseus, a mortal hero, blinded him. Poseidon got mad. He tortured Odysseus for many years. Poseidon created storms and earthquakes. He wrecked Odysseus's ships. He killed Odysseus's shipmates. He turned one of

Today, we know that earthquakes are not caused by Poseidon.

Real World Connection

Triton was Poseidon's son. Triton was the messenger of the sea. He was a merman. He had the upper body of a man. He had the lower body of a fish. Eric Ducharme has been obsessed with mermaids since he was young. He makes fake mermaid fins. He slips into his fish tails. He swims around Florida's waterways. He calls this "mermaiding." It's his own style of costumed free-diving. He said, "I do eat, breathe, and sleep mermaids. It's my lifestyle. It's the path in life that I have chosen. ... When I put on a tail, I feel transformed. I feel like I'm starting to enter into a different world when I hit the water." He holds his breath for four minutes at a time.

Triton is the son of Poseidon and Amphitrite.
He lived with them in an underwater palace.

Odysseus's ships into stone. He sent sea monsters.

Poseidon was also jealous. He was greedy. He fought other gods. He fought mortals. He wanted control. He wanted power.

Poseidon also messed with the mind. Some mortals **displeased** him. They made him mad. They didn't do what he wanted. So, he'd strike them with **epilepsy**.

Epilepsy is when people have **seizures** or shakes. Some people screamed like a horse. Poseidon was believed to cause this type of epilepsy.

Poseidon was **immortal**. This means he lived forever. He was hard to defeat. It was best to stay out of his way.

Polybotes was a giant born to fight Poseidon. Poseidon buried Polybotes under the island of Cos.

CHAPTER 4

TRIDENTS AND CHARIOTS, OH MY!

What are Poseidon's weapons? What is a chariot?
What is Atlantis?

During the war against the Titans, Poseidon and his brothers saved the **Cyclopes**. Cyclopes were giants. They each had one eye. They were imprisoned. They were grateful to be released. They gave each brother a weapon. Zeus chose a thunderbolt. Hades chose a helmet of darkness. Poseidon chose a **trident**. Tridents are spears. They have three prongs. They look like sharp forks.

He'd point his trident into the sea. This created storms. He'd point his trident into the air. This raised winds.

He'd point his trident onto the land. This created earthquakes. He also used his trident to bring water out of the ground. He created springs and streams.

Poseidon rode his **chariot**. A chariot is a cart. It has two wheels. It was used in war and racing.

Poseidon and his brothers used their weapons to defeat the Titans.

The animals that pulled Poseidon's chariot were called hippocampuses.

Poseidon's chariot was made of gold. He rode it through the waves. It was pulled by strange animals. The animals were half-horse and half-fish. They looked like horses with fish tails.

Fish and dolphins swam with him. They swam beside him. They followed his chariot.

Cross-Cultural Connection

Aztecs were ancient people. They lived in central Mexico. They worshipped gods similar to Poseidon. Chalchiuhlatonal was a god of water. He looked over the sea. He protected sea animals. He had a human take care of the sea. In exchange, he gave the human the gift of water. He was related to Chalchiuhtlicue. Chalchiuhtlicue was a goddess of groundwater. She was connected to rivers, lakes, springs, and streams. She was known as "she of the jade skirt." She was youthful and beautiful. She helped women give birth. She protected children. She helped crops grow. She's known for causing a great flood. She saved humans by turning them into fish. She created a bridge linking Earth to heaven to save those she liked.

Poseidon kept his chin up high. He rode fast. He surfed the waves. He marked his territory. He let everyone know he owned the seas.

Each god had a city. The god protected the city. In turn, the city honored the god. Poseidon wanted a city.

He mated with a human princess. Her name was Cleito. He protected her. He built her a castle. It was on a faraway island. It was on top of a hill. Rings of land and water surrounded it. The island always had water. It always had food.

They had 10 sons. Atlas was their first son. He was the first king of the island. The island was named Atlantis. Atlantis was peaceful for many years. Poseidon was proud.

But future generations didn't worship Poseidon. Poseidon became angry. He created a flood. He created an earthquake. He sank Atlantis under the ocean.

Poseidon had a hard time finding a city to honor him because of his temper.

CHAPTER 5

BEWARE OF THE ANGRY SEA-GOD

Why did Poseidon create the Minotaur? Why does Poseidon dislike the city of Troy?

There are many myths about Poseidon.

Crete is a Greek island. King Minos ruled it. He wanted a gift. Poseidon gave him his best bull. King Minos was supposed to **sacrifice** it. This means to honor the gods by giving up a life. But King Minos liked the bull. He kept it for himself. He sacrificed his own bull instead. Poseidon got angry. He made the king's wife fall in love with the bull. The bull and the queen had a child. The child had a bull's head and tail. But it had a human body. It was called the Minotaur. It was kept in a maze under the castle.

Greece was at war with Troy for many years. Troy was a city in Turkey. Poseidon was sent to help Troy. Troy's king asked Poseidon to build a wall around the city. The wall was for protection. The king promised Poseidon a gift. He didn't keep his promise. Poseidon got mad. He punished the king.

Aphrodite, the goddess of love, sometimes helped Poseidon get even.

He sent a sea monster.

Poseidon then supported Greece in the war. He stayed angry at Troy's king.

Explained By Science

Potidaea was a small Greek village. The Persian army tried to invade it in 479 BCE. But a huge wave came. It washed away hundreds of Persian soldiers. It saved the town. Herodotus was a Greek historian. He believed Poseidon sent the crushing wave to punish the Persians. Today's scientists explained that a tsunami killed the Persians, not Poseidon. Herodotus described the phases of a tsunami, not an act of a god. A tsunami is a large ocean wave. It's caused by an underwater earthquake. It's also caused by volcano explosions. Huge amounts of water are displaced. Water surges upward. Then it falls back. A series of waves are formed. Tsunamis are also called wave trains.

The gods split their loyalties between Greece and Troy.

Don't anger the gods. Poseidon had great powers. And he knew how to use them.

DID YOU KNOW?

- Roman myths have a sea god. His name is Neptune. He's the Roman version of Poseidon.

- Poseidon had several other names. He has been called "Holder of the Earth," "Earth-Shaker," and "Tamer of Horses."

- Poseidon's wife, Amphitrite, was jealous. She didn't like Poseidon's girlfriends. She could be mean. For example, she poisoned Scylla. Scylla was a pretty sea nymph. Amphitrite threw magical herbs in her bath. Scylla turned into an ugly sea monster. She had six heads. She had three rows of teeth. She had 12 feet. She sounded like yelping dogs. She ate sailors.

- Poseidon was father of Theseus. Theseus was the king of Athens. He was famous for slaying the Minotaur.

- Ancient Greeks respected the sea. They were great explorers. Their ships sailed to distant places. Because of this, Poseidon was an important god.

- Zeus was depicted as the firstborn son. Poseidon was actually born before Zeus. But the beginning of Poseidon's life was spent inside his father's stomach. So, his rebirth made him younger than Zeus.

- Sailors prayed to Poseidon. They wanted a safe voyage. Some sailors drowned horses as a sacrifice.

- Poseidon traveled in water. But he didn't get wet.

CONSIDER THIS!

TAKE A POSITION Read the other 45th Parallel Press books about Zeus and Hades. Which god do you think was the most important? Argue your point with reasons and evidence.

SAY WHAT? Stories about gods and goddesses explain events in nature. List at least three natural events attributed to Poseidon. Explain how Poseidon caused these events.

THINK ABOUT IT! Poseidon had different powers. Which of Poseidon's powers would you like to have? Why? What would you do with this power? Would you use this power for good or evil?

LEARN MORE

Hoena, B. A. *Poseidon*. Mankato, MN: Capstone Press, 2004.

O'Connor, George. *Poseidon: Earth Shaker*. New York: Roaring Brook Press, 2013.

Temple, Teri, and Robert Squier (illustrator). *Poseidon: God of the Sea and Earthquakes*. North Mankato, MN: The Child's World, 2013.

GLOSSARY

chariot (CHAR-ee-uht) two-wheeled cart

Cyclopes (SYE-klop-eez) giants with one eye

displeased (dis-PLEEZD) to make someone upset or angry or disappointed

epilepsy (EP-uh-lep-see) nerve disorder in which people convulse or blank out

eroded (ih-RODE-id) to wear away

immortal (ih-MOR-tuhl) to live forever

moody (MOO-dee) often changing moods

mortals (MOR-tuhlz) humans

nymph (NIMF) spirit

Olympians (uh-LIM-pee-uhnz) rulers of the gods who live on Mount Olympus

revenge (rih-VENJ) to get even

sacrifice (SAK-ruh-fise) to offer a life

seizures (SEE-zhurz) convulsions or shakes

siblings (SIB-lingz) brothers and sisters

temper (TEM-pur) angry state of mind

Titans (TYE-tunz) giant gods who ruled before the Olympians

trident (TRYE-dent) three-pronged spear

INDEX

JAN 2018